Contents

Early Railways

Early seventeenth century mine-owners realised that horses could pull heavier loads more quickly on wooden tracks than on the pot-holed, muddy roads that were usual for the day. By 1750, over 150 kilometres of these wooden wagonways had been built. After this time, iron rails were used; these were harder and so wore more slowly. This picture, drawn in 1773, shows coal being taken down to ships from a mine.

Steam engines were being used in mines at this time, but were fixed to one spot and used to pump water. It wasn't until 1803 that Richard Trevithick combined steam engines and rails. The **railway** was born. The Surrey Iron Railway, opened in 1804, was perhaps the first public line in the country.

Other engineers developed Trevithick's work. In 1814 George Stephenson ran his first steam engine — the 'Blucher'. It pulled eight heavy wagons at 6 kph. In 1825, his 'Locomotion' pulled more than 90 tonnes at 18 kph along the Stockton to Darlington railway.

Stephenson's most famous engine, the 'Rocket', was built to enter a competition to find the best engine for a new railway line linking Liverpool to Manchester. Stephenson's engine won the £500 prize, the two other competing engines broke down.

Stephenson's 'Rocket'

Funnel
Boiler
Piston
Coal
Water
Driving wheel
Connecting Rod
Firebox
Tender

SURREY Iron Railway.

The COMMITTEE of the SURREY IRON RAILWAY COMPANY,

HEREBY, GIVE NOTICE,. That the BASON at *Wandsworth*, and the Railway therefrom up to *Croydon* and *Carfhalton*, is now open for the Ufe of the Public, on Payment of the following Tolls, *viz.*

For all Coals entering into or going out of their Bason at Wandsworth,	*per Chaldron,*	3d.
For all other Goods entering into or going out of their Bason at Wandsworth -	*per Ton,*	3d.

For all GOODS carried on the said RAILWAY, as follows, viz.

For Dung, - - -	*per Ton, per Mile,*	1d.
For Lime, and all Manures, (except Dung,) Lime-ftone, Chalk, Clay, Breeze, Afhes, Sand, Bricks, Stone, Flints, and Fuller's Earth,	*per Ton, per Mile,*	2d.
For Coals, - - -	*per Chald. per Mile,*	3d.
And, For all other Goods, -	*per Ton, per Mile,*	3d.

By ORDER of the COMMITTEE,

W. B. LUTTLY,
Clerk of the Company.

Wandsworth, June 1, 1804.

BROOKE, PRINTER, No. 35, PATERNOSTER-ROW, LONDON.

Activities

A 1 Look at the diagram of the 'Rocket'. Try to explain how it works.
   2 Look up Stockton and Darlington, and Liverpool and Manchester, in an atlas. Then work out how far it was on each line.

John Corn

Arnold-Wheaton
A Division of E. J. Arnold & Son Limited
Parkside Lane, Leeds LS11 5TD

A member of the Pergamon Group
Headington Hill Hall, Oxford OX3 0BW

ISBN 0 560-26539-5

First published 1987
Printed in Great Britain by A. Wheaton & Co. Ltd.,
Hennock Road, Exeter

ACKNOWLEDGEMENTS

The author and publisher wish to thank the following for permission to reproduce material in this book:

Bluebell Railway Ltd.
British Rail — Eastern Region
Ceefax Ltd.
Channel Tunnel Group
Dart Valley Light Railway plc
Ffestiniog Railway
Keighley and Worth Valley Railway
Kent & East Sussex Railway
North York Moors Historical Railway Trust
Science Museum — London
Severn Valley Railway
Strathspey Railway Co. Ltd.
West Somerset Railway
York Railway Museum

Cover photograph: Jock Graham

Illustration and layout by Terry Bambrook

Railway lines were built by gangs of men called **navvies**. They hacked out tunnels and cuttings, and built embankments and bridges using only basic tools and muscle power. Their lives were hard. Often they worked for up to 16 hours a day and seven days a week in all weathers. The work was very badly paid. Look at the table showing a navvy's daily wages.

Date	Railway Line	Daily Wage
1822-27	Stockton-Darlington	7½-17½p
1848	Huddersfield-Manchester	14p
1861	S. Durham and Lancashire Union	19p
1869	Settle-Carlisle	20p
1900	Ballachulish	21p

B **1** Work out how much a navvy would have earned each week working on these railway lines.
2 Look at the sketch of a navvy. Make a list of his work tools and what he would use each for.

The navvies lived alongside the track in **shants** — collections of wooden or **sod** huts. The shants were cramped and dirty, so diseases such as typhus and cholera were common. The sod huts were worst of all. These were made of turf with planks across the top forming a roof. One sod hut, by the Edinburgh to Hawick line, in 1846, measured 8 by 4 metres and housed 20 people. Children slept in a meat safe slung from the rafters in another shant; on the Kettering to Manton line this was called the **brat cage**.

Even though they were the object of contempt by local people for their violence and drunkenness, the navvies accomplished extraordinary feats, including the construction of 32,000 km of track in the nineteenth century across all kinds of barriers.

Activities

C **1** In what ways did navvies have a hard life?
2 Do you think that railway contractors, the people who organized railway building, should have improved the conditions of the navvies?
What improvements should they have made?

Investigating

Railway Building

The early nineteenth century saw a huge increase in industrial activity. With this came the need for good transport links to get raw materials to factories and finished goods to markets. This led to a great expansion in the railway network. Many new lines were built to connect towns and ports to factories and coalfields. But railway building is not easy, trains can only manage gentle slopes of about 2% (two metres in every 100), and so a lot of land had to be altered in order that lines could be built.

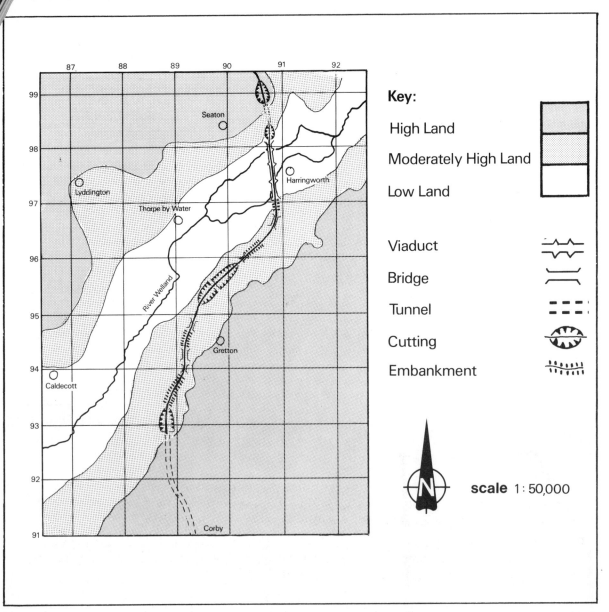

Key:

High Land

Moderately High Land

Low Land

Viaduct

Bridge

Tunnel

Cutting

Embankment

scale 1 : 50,000

The map on page 6 shows part of the Kettering to Manton railway line. A lot of work had to be done to keep the railway line more or less level. Look at this chart:

Line Kettering to Manton	Ref. 9099 to 8991	Section length 12 km		
Feature	Number	Sketch	Ref.	Notes
Viaducts	1		9097	A very long viaduct built of brick. It has 82 arches and is about 18 m high. It is just over 1 km long.
Bridges	ⅢⅡ		9096 9096 8994 8994 8993	One of the bridges is made of brick, the others are made of stone.
Cuttings	ⅢⅡ		9099 9098 8995 8995 8893	Cuttings can be found near the tunnels and to the north of Gretton.
Embankments	IIII		9096 9096 8994 8893	There are four embankments along the line. The embankment at 8893 is very high.
Tunnels	II		9098 8991	One short tunnel and one very long one north of Corby. This tunnel is nearly 2 km long and about 35 m below ground.
Total	17			

Activities

A 1 How long is this stretch of railway line?
 2 Which are the most common structures? Why do you think there are so many of these?
 3 Which feature do you think was most difficult to build?
 4 On what sort of ground will you find the fewest or most simple structures?

B Conduct an investigation on a stretch of railway line near your school. On a chart like the one above, record the features that you find; a 1:50,000 map will help. Visit the line and draw or photograph some of the features that are there.

Victorian Railways

The first half of the nineteenth century saw a massive increase in railway building. The flamboyant Victorians built elegant stations to celebrate the new railway age. Before railways, working people rarely ventured beyond their own town or village. Coach travel had always been slow and expensive, but railways changed all that. Day trips to the coast became very popular and towns like Brighton, Scarborough and Blackpool grew quickly.

Many railway companies began to organize excursions to race meetings, cricket matches, or the coast, and built their own hotels offering excellent accommodation and service.

Activities

A Look at the chart showing railway use.
1 Draw a bar graph to show these figures.
2 Over which years did railway use grow most quickly?

Rail passengers 1841-1891

Year	Million passengers carried
1841	7.5
1851	79.0
1861	163.0
1871	359.0
1881	608.0
1891	823.0

Trains were often crowded and uncomfortable, and sometimes unreliable and dangerous. However, conditions did improve as rival companies fought for larger shares of passengers.

B Below is a copy of a painting showing Paddington station in 1862.
1 Where is the luggage stored? How is that different from today?
2 How does this station scene compare with a modern one? Use some of the photographs later on in the book to help you.

Journeys by rail were very different from those of today. Look at these two sets of information to compare a mid-Victorian journey with a modern one.

1854 A SPECIAL TRAIN will leave the undermentioned Stations for London, as		
A Northern Railway Excursion to London and the Crystal Palace	TIME OF STARTING.	Fares to LONDON
	A.M.	FIRST CLASS. s. d.
York . . . dep.	10.15	37 6
Church Fenton . . "	10.35	34 6
Milford Junction . . "	10.55	33 6
Halifax . . . "	9.20	34 6
Bradford . . . "	9.30	34 6
Leeds (Marsh Lane) . "	10.15	34 6
Wakefield . . . "	10.15	34 0
Pontefract . . . "	10.40	32 0
Knottingley . . arr.	11.10	32 0
Ditto . . . dep.	11.15	
Askerne . . . "	11.30	31 0
Doncaster . . arr.	11.45	30 0
Ditto . . . dep.	11.55	
Bawtry . . . "	12.10	27 3
Retford . . "	12.35	25 9
Sheffield (regular train) . "	11. 0	31 6
Traxford . . . "	12.30	25 0
Newark . . "	1.15	25 0
Nottingham (regular train) . "	12. 0	25 0
Grantham . . . "	1.50	20 0
Stamford . . . "	1.30	17 3
Tallington . . . "	2.30	15 9
Peterborough . . arr.	2.50	14 3
Ditto . . . dep.	3.10	
Hitchin . . . "	4.45	. .
London (King's Cross) . arr.	6. 0	. .

Town	Dep. Time	Return Fare £	
		First	Second
York	1426	77.00	51.0
Doncaster	1448	66.00	43.00
Retford	1503	54.60	35.36
Newark	1518	47.40	31.00
Grantham	1531	41.00	26.60
Peterborough	1600	33.20	21.40
Huntingdon	1616	23.00	14.60
Stevenage	1641	12.80	8.60
London (King's Cross)	arrive 1701	Destination London	London

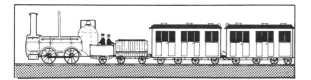

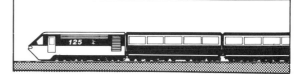

C 1 Work out the time taken to travel from York to London in 1854. How long would this journey take today?
2 Why do you think the Victorian train stopped for some time at Knottingley, Doncaster and Peterborough? (Hint: there were no corridors on these trains).
3 It is about 320 km from York to London. Try to work out the average speed of the 1854 train and the modern train.
4 Write a paragraph comparing the Victorian and the modern journeys.

Things to think about
What advantages do you think the modern trains have over the Victorian ones?

Investigating

Victorian Stations

The early nineteenth century saw an enormous increase in railway building; new lines meant new stations in the towns, and often villages, they passed through. Some stations were imposing and included a railway hotel, but even the smallest was clean and well run. Stations today have a different character from those of 100 years ago.

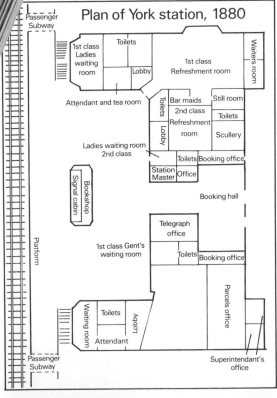

Plan of York station, 1880

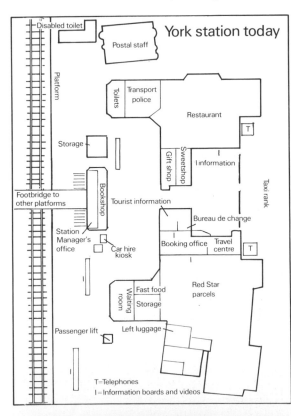

York station today

Look at these plans and photographs of York station. The platform photographs are taken from the same position. What similarities and differences do you notice?

Activities

A   Copy and complete these charts to show the changes at York Station.

Plan	Comfort	Administration, offices	Others
Buildings, rooms there in 1880			
Building, room there today			
Buildings, rooms doing the same job in the same place in 1880 and today			

Photograph	1880	Today
Buildings		
People		
Trains		

B   **1** What things have disappeared from York station since the 1880s?
2 Write a paragraph saying how the station has changed over the last 100 years.

C   Investigate how a station near you has changed. Visit your local library and try to find out what the station was like in the past. Look for old photographs, plans and accounts of station life. Elderly people may provide useful information. Visit the station yourself, collect information of the same type, then compare the two sets.

Rail Cuts and Changes

Shortly after the railways were nationalized in 1948, they reached a crisis. The country had inherited too much track, too many railway workers and too many out of date engines — the railways were losing passengers, freight and money. Changes had to be made. In 1962 Dr. Beeching was appointed to modernize the railways — he proposed sweeping changes in his report the following year.

The British Railways network before the changes made by Dr. Beeching

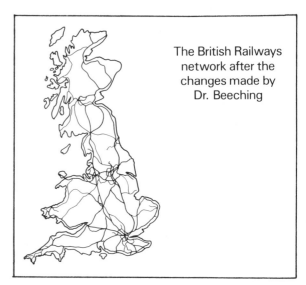

The British Railways network after the changes made by Dr. Beeching

Activities

A 1 What happened to the length of track under Dr. Beeching's proposals?

2 From what kind of areas do you think track was lost?

B Track length was not the only thing to feel the effect of Dr. Beeching's 'axe'; all areas of railway life were cut back.

1 Draw bar graphs, using these charts, to show the effects of Dr. Beeching's changes.

2 How do you think these changes altered the railway system?

Graph showing length of track against year

Year	Passenger stations	Marshalling yards
1938	6698	1016
1951	6214	958
1963	4306	602
1982	2369	59

Year	Railway employees
1938	581401
1951	599890
1967	279371
1972	229636
1982	161407

A further transformation in the railways was the phasing out of steam trains, with diesel trains being introduced to replace them. The last main line steam train ran on the 11th August, 1968.

> **C** **1** Why do you think steam locomotives were phased out?
> **2** What disadvantages did they have compared with diesel?

Dr. Beeching did help railways to improve in terms of comfort and speed. There were also improvements in freight handling, signalling and track replacment. Even so, in some parts of the country Dr. Beeching had few friends.

> **D** **1** What sorts of people do you think objected to Dr. Beeching's cuts?
> **2** Write a letter to Dr. Beeching complaining about the closure of your local station — write about the effect it will have on your way of life.

Dr. Beeching's proposals resulted in thousands of empty station buildings, and thousands of kilometres of railway lines being removed. Some station buildings were demolished or left to decay, some were bought and converted into houses or factories. The paths of some old railway tracks have been reclaimed for farmland or used as building land, other paths have just remained derelict. A few local councils have converted old tracks into cycleways or walkways. An example of this is the Tissington Trail in the Peak District National Park. The Trail is about 20 kilometres long and follows the old Buxton to Ashbourne railway line.

> **Things to think about**
> What do you think old railway lines and station buildings could be used for?

Investigating
Local Rail Cuts

The Beeching proposals closed many stations throughout the country; very few areas were left unaffected. Look at this map of Northamptonshire:

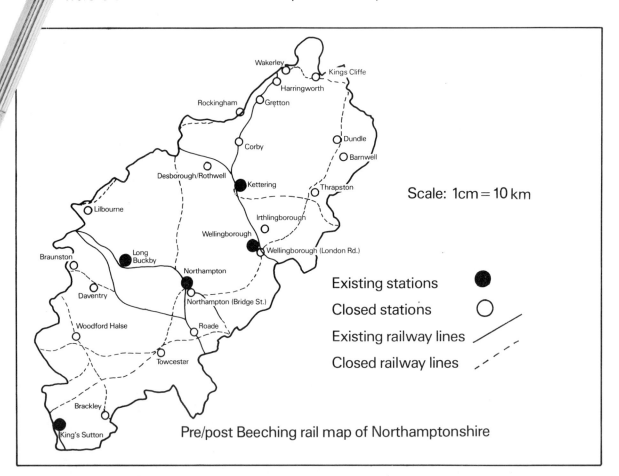

Scale: 1cm = 10 km

Existing stations ●
Closed stations ○
Existing railway lines ——
Closed railway lines ----

Pre/post Beeching rail map of Northamptonshire

Activities

A
1 How many stations in Northamptonshire were closed by Dr. Beeching?
2 Use a strip of paper to measure the length of track removed after his proposals.
3 How much track and how many stations remain?
4 Make two lists, one showing closed stations, the other showing stations remaining open.

B Investigate the changes made in your county or local area in the wake of the Beeching report.
On an outline map, mark in working and disused stations. Plot existing and old track. Use a colour code. A 1:50,000 or 1:100,000 scale map will help you.
Try to answer the question in part A again, using your locality.

After 1963 many station buildings found new uses, some were sold and converted into houses or factories, others were either demolished or left to decay. The chart below shows what happened to stations in one particular area.

County/area _East of County_	
Station	**New use Comments**
1	House – with a garage
2	Factory – makes clothes
3	Demolished – no sign of old station
4	House – with a small garden
5	Demolished – both platforms remain
6	House – waiting rooms on the old platforms are now sheds
7	Factory – makes electrical goods. Railway line still used
8	House – station is a house, platform area is a scrap yard
9	Demolished – nothing left at all
10	House – very large garden
11	Derelict – old station is still there but falling down

C 1 What has happened to most of the station buildings?
2 Draw a simple bar graph to show the results.
3 Try to find out what has happened to the stations in your area.
Make a chart like this one.

The station shown here once served a village called Rockingham in Northamptonshire. The station is now a house and boarding kennels.

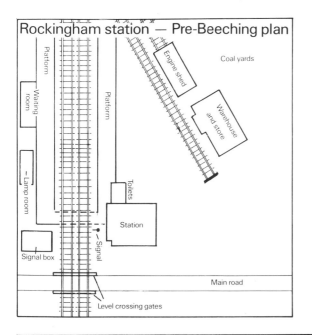

Rockingham station — Pre-Beeching plan

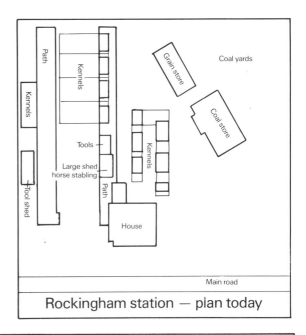

Rockingham station — plan today

D 1 How has the Rockingham station changed since 1963?
2 Make a thorough investigation of a disused station near your school. On your visit, photograph or sketch the old station. Draw a plan and label it, and record any evidence of any cargo areas and outbuildings. Talk to old people to find out what they remember of the station.

Railway Safety and Maintenance

Early trains were notoriously dangerous. Brakes were generally poor, and signalling was often little better than guesswork. In one week in 1845, there were 17 accidents. One cartoon of the time suggested that travellers should take with them a set of surgical instruments and directions for making a will! Improvements in safety were urgently needed, and slowly they came. The **block** system of signalling was a major technical advance. The railway line was divided into blocks and only one train was allowed into a block at any one time. The signalman, in his box, kept in touch with other signalmen with the new electric telegraph, so information about train movements could be passed down the line. Signalmen had to watch the line and change semaphore signals by pulling huge levers. There are still many of these signal boxes today.

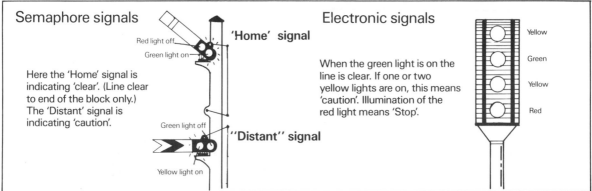

Semaphore signals

Red light off
Green light on

'Home' signal

Here the 'Home' signal is indicating 'clear'. (Line clear to end of the block only.) The 'Distant' signal is indicating 'caution'.

Green light off

"Distant" signal

Yellow light on

Electronic signals

When the green light is on the line is clear. If one or two yellow lights are on, this means 'caution'. Illumination of the red light means 'Stop'.

Yellow
Green
Yellow
Red

Nowadays signalling is done by electronics. Coloured lights on display boards show the movement of trains. Signals and points are altered by the flick of a switch. New, high visibility signal lights are able to penetrate darkness and fog, and are much easier for drivers to see.

Activities

A 1 Why do you think improvements in safety were slow to come?
   2 How is the job of a signal operator easier today than it was in the past?

Train drivers can also be warned of danger by the **Automatic Warning System** (AWS). This device is fitted to over 8,500 kilometres of track — it makes a *horn* sound in the driver's cab if a distant signal is at caution. The driver has seven seconds to brake, otherwise the brakes are applied automatically. A *bell* sounds if the track is clear, but this again has to be cancelled or the brakes will be applied automatically.

B Why should the brakes be applied if the driver fails to react to the horn?

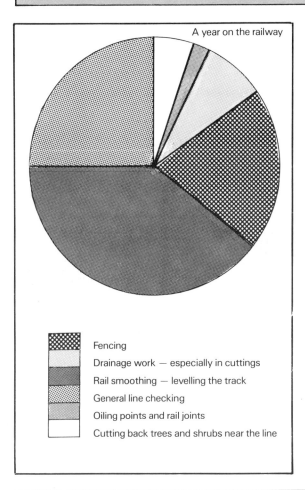

A year on the railway

Fencing

Drainage work — especially in cuttings

Rail smoothing — levelling the track

General line checking

Oiling points and rail joints

Cutting back trees and shrubs near the line

Most of the responsibility for keeping the track in good order rests with the railway workers. These workers have a variety of jobs to do. Look at this pie chart and key.

C 1 Rank the jobs that railway workers do; start with the most important.
2 Which job takes the most time?
3 Why is fencing so important?

The railway workers in this photograph are concerned for their own safety. This is some of the equipment they take with them: bright over-vests, whistles, air horns, flags, detonators.

D 1 Suggest why each piece of equipment should be taken by the railway workers.
Make a chart to show your answers.
2 The station manager is ultimately responsible for railway safety on and around the station. Look at this drawing to see if you can find out what he does.

Things to think about
Railways are the safest way to travel. Can you think of any ways that they could be made even safer?
Design a poster to advertise your best idea.

Investigating
Railway Maintenance

"We are sorry for the delay of the 12.35 to Nottingham. This is due to..." Have you ever heard an announcement like this? For the Inter-City network to be speedy, efficient and safe, it must all be working properly all of the time. It is such a complex system that this is rarely the case. Modern technology can be used to see where any trouble lies.

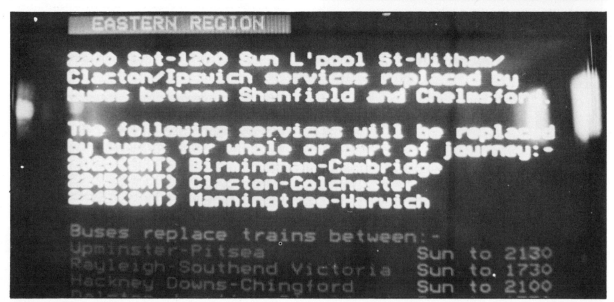

Information about rail problems can be obtained by looking at Ceefax pages. Page one of news concerning the Eastern Region can be seen in the photograph above; the final page, page two, is shown here.

0800 to 1600 Sunday services between King's Cross and Peterborough diverted with 20 minutes delay.

2230 Saturday to 1330 Sunday services between Doncaster and Peterborough diverted.
Rail/road connections to/from Grantham, Newark and Retford.

2300 Saturday to 0500 Monday services will not call at Wakefield. Rail connections to/from Wakefield.

Sunday 1000 to 1500 buses to replace trains between Sheffield and Dore.

A group of children completed this chart, based upon problems on the Eastern Region over one weekend.

News number/ Rail service		Cancellation — why?	Delays — how long/why?	Buses replace — from/to	Diversions — to where?	Stations missed	Other reason
1	Liverpool Street – Clacton/Ipswich	–	–	✓ Sherfield to Chelmsford	– ●	–	–
2	Birmingham – Cambridge	–	–	✓ –	–	–	–
3	Clacton – Colchester	–	–	✓ –	–	–	–
4	Manningtree – Harwich	–	–	✓ –	–	–	–
5	Upminster – Pitsea	–	–	✓ –	–	–	–
6	Rayleigh – Southend	–	–	✓ –	–	–	–
7	Hackney Downs – Chingford	–	–	✓ –	–	–	–
8	Dalston Junction – Stratford	–	–	✓	–	–	–
9	Kings Cross – Peterborough	–	20 mins	–	✓ –	–	–
10	Peterborough – Doncaster	–	–	✓ Grantham/ Newark/Retford	✓ –	–	–
11	All Inter-Cities via Wakefield	–	–	–	–	Wakefield	–
12	Sheffield – Dore	–	–	✓ –	–	–	–

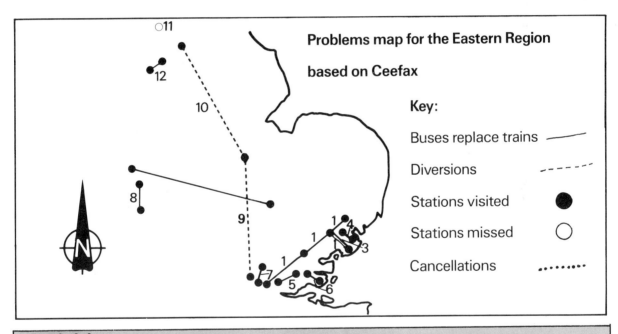

Problems map for the Eastern Region based on Ceefax

Key:

Buses replace trains ——

Diversions - - - - - -

Stations visited ●

Stations missed ○

Cancellations ·········

Activities

A Look at the chart and map above.
   1 Is there any area of the Eastern Region which seems to be especially hard hit?
   2 How many services were diverted?
   3 What other form of transport does British Rail use in order to help overcome problems?
   4 What could passengers from Wakefield do if they wanted to travel by train the weekend the chart was made?

B 1 Complete an investigation into rail problems in your region, using either Ceefax or Oracle. Show your results on a chart like the one above, and make a map with a key.
   2 How does your information compare with the information on this page?
   3 Did you have any especially interesting rail news?

Train Journeys

Think carefully. Have you ever travelled by train? If you have, you would have needed to buy a ticket. By looking at a ticket, we can find out a lot about how and why people travel by train. Look at this ticket and see what you can find out about it.

Activities

A 1 Where is the ticket to?
2 How much did it cost?
3 When was it bought?
4 When during the week did the passenger want to travel?
5 What is the 'class' of the ticket?
6 Make a list of the places that you have been to by train.
Put them on a map.

It is wise to look at a timetable before travelling to check departure and arrival times. Timetables are available at every station; they may be displayed as posters or on video screens. Look at this timetable extract showing departures from York to Cardiff.

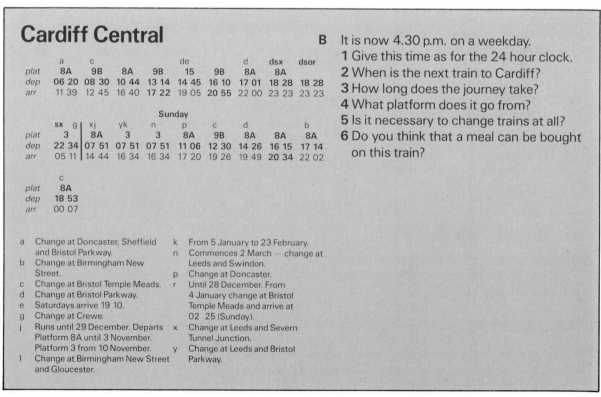

Cardiff Central

	a	c			de		d	dsx	dsor
plat	8A	9B	8A	9B	15	9B	8A	8A	
dep	06 20	08 30	10 44	13 14	14 45	16 10	17 01	18 28	18 28
arr	11 39	12 45	16 40	17 22	19 05	20 55	22 00	23 23	23 23

Sunday

	sx	g	xj	yk	n	p	c	d		b
plat	3	8A	07 51	3	3	8A	9B	8A	8A	8A
dep	22 34	07 51	07 51	07 51	11 06	12 30	14 26	16 15	17 14	
arr	05 11	14 44	16 34	16 34	17 20	19 26	19 49	20 34	22 02	

	c
plat	8A
dep	18 53
arr	00 07

a Change at Doncaster, Sheffield and Bristol Parkway.
b Change at Birmingham New Street.
c Change at Bristol Temple Meads.
d Change at Bristol Parkway.
e Saturdays arrive 19 10.
g Change at Crewe.
j Runs until 29 December. Departs Platform 8A until 3 November. Platform 3 from 10 November.
l Change at Birmingham New Street and Gloucester.
k From 5 January to 23 February.
n Commences 2 March — change at Leeds and Swindon.
p Change at Doncaster.
r Until 28 December. From 4 January change at Bristol Temple Meads and arrive at 02 25 (Sunday).
x Change at Leeds and Severn Tunnel Junction.
y Change at Leeds and Bristol Parkway.

B It is now 4.30 p.m. on a weekday.
1 Give this time as for the 24 hour clock.
2 When is the next train to Cardiff?
3 How long does the journey take?
4 What platform does it go from?
5 Is it necessary to change trains at all?
6 Do you think that a meal can be bought on this train?

All train journeys begin and end at a station. People travelling on unfamiliar journeys need two things from stations to make their journeys more pleasant — comfort (somewhere to rest or eat) and information (so that they can catch the right train from the correct platform).

Most rail passengers today are commuters — people travelling to and from work. They are carried on either suburban or Inter-City trains. The Inter-City network covers the main towns and cities of mainland Britain, providing fast and efficient links across the country.

This map shows routes and train times to London, the workplace of millions of people. Most commuters are prepared to spend 1 to 1½ hours each day travelling to work.

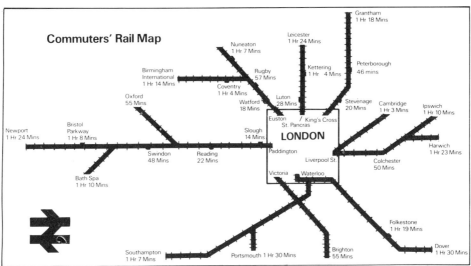

Commuters' Rail Map

COMFORT	INFORMATION

C In this photograph, there are many things designed for passenger comfort and information. See if you can spot them. Make a chart like this one to show your results.

D **1** How many towns and cities are within commutable distance of London?
2 Mark these places on a map. Join together places within 30 minutes of London, between 30 minutes and 1 hour, and between 1 and 1½ hours of London. Use different colours.

Things to think about
1 What would you like to see in your station to help passengers pass the time between connections?
2 What are the advantages and disadvantages of commuting long distances to work each day?

Investigating

Train Journeys

Here are the details of a railway journey from York to Great Yarmouth. Work out how much time is spent travelling and how much waiting.

York	Peterborough	Norwich	Great Yarmouth
dep: 1544	arrive: 1703	arrive: 2023	
	dep: 1839	dep: 2100	arrive: 2130

Travellers expect to spend their waiting time comfortably, safe in the knowledge that they will catch the right connection!

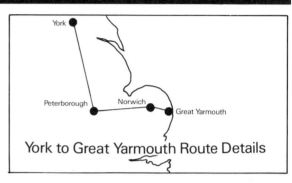

York to Great Yarmouth Route Details

A group of children did a survey of their local station to see how well it cared for passengers. Look at the chart they completed.

Station Bradfield		
Comfort facility	**Score 0-5**	**Comments**
Station cleanliness	3	Some litter bins are overflowing
Waiting room	4	Small but very comfortable
Refreshments	2	Sweets and crisps only
Bookstall	0	None at all
Luggage trolleys	2	A few – in poor condition
Seating	3	Adequate seating
Toilets	5	Very clean and for disabled passengers
Left luggage	0	No facilities
Telephones	1	Only one telephone
Others, please list:		
Information facility checklist		
Poster timetable	✓	Plenty – well displayed
Video timetable	—	None
Announcer	—	None
Enquiry office	✓	At ticket office
Information person	—	None
Interview 1	'Everything is very good but a bookstall would be nice.'	
Interview 2	'More care should be taken cleaning up – there's too much litter.'	
Interview 3	'There doesn't seem to be much to do when you're waiting for a train.'	

Activities

A
1. What was the total score for comfort items? Is this good or bad do you think?
2. What comfort items needed improving?
3. Do you think that the station is well looked after?
4. How many sources of information were there?
5. Were the passengers happy with the facilities at Bradfield station?
6. Do you think that Bradfield is a small or large station? Give your reasons.

B Conduct an investigation at your local main line station to see what facilities are provided for passengers. Use a survey sheet like the one above. Score the quality of the facilities from 0-5: 0=very poor or non-existent, 5=excellent. Interview passengers to discover their views on your local station. If you can, map the location of comfort and information facilities on a plan of the station.

Where can you get to direct from your station? A look at the station's poster timetable will tell you.

C **1** Visit your local station and make a list of the places you can get to without changing trains. If it is a large station, divide into four groups for destinations A-F, G-L, M-R and S-Z.

2 At school, put a piece of tracing paper over an atlas map, label your station and plot the different destinations with coloured dots. If you are working in four groups, pass your group's tracing paper around the class for other groups to add their results.

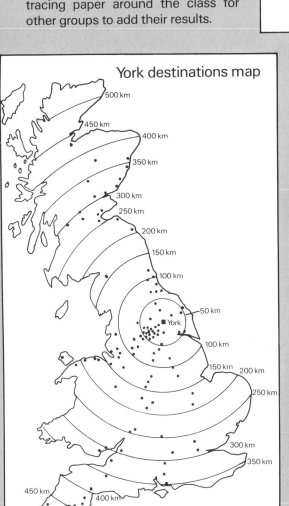

York destinations map

D This map has been drawn showing towns with direct rail links to York. Lines have been added to the map at 50 kilometre intervals.

1 Count the number of destinations within each zone and copy and complete this chart.

Distance from York km	Destinations
0-50	
50-100	
100-150	
150-200	
200-250	
250-300	
300-350	
350-400	
400+	

2 Draw a bar graph to show your results.
3 What do you notice about the number of direct rail links from York the further away you travel?

E **1** Draw a map and complete a chart like those above, to show direct links from your station. Use them to construct a bar graph.
2 Answer question 3 again using information from your station.

Railways Past Present and Future

Steam trains have not been allowed to die away completely. The National Railway Museum in York has exhibits dating from 1829. Since it opened in 1975, over 13 million people have visited the museum. A few of the exhibits are in working order, but the true working railway museums are run by Preservation Societies, which operate stretches of private line.

Activities

A **1** Why do you think that only a few museum exhibits are in working order?
2 Do you have a private railway near your school?

Today, British Rail is spending a lot of money on the electrification of lines. They believe that it is an important step forward. Look at these arguments for and against electrification.

For
1 Locomotives are cleaner.
2 Speeds are easily maintained.
3 Running costs are less.
4 Less air pollution.

Against
1 Very expensive to install — £300,000 per kilometre.
2 Only worthwhile to electrify important lines.
3 Overhead lines are not pleasant to look at

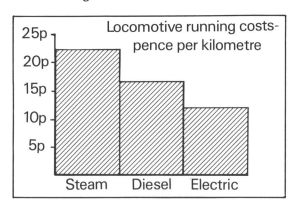

Locomotive running costs- pence per kilometre

B After looking at the arguments for and against electrification, do you think that British Rail's scheme is a good idea?

This map shows British Rail's plans for the electrification of the East Coast main line. The line is about 560 kilometres long and will cost £300 million to electrify. The scheme will involve the construction of 32,000 masts to support the 2,500 kilometres of overhead wires. This will mean the raising or rebuilding of 130 bridges.

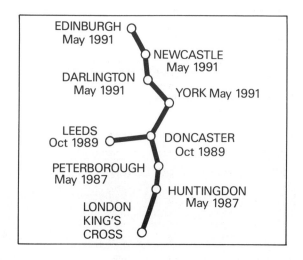

EDINBURGH
May 1991

NEWCASTLE
May 1991

DARLINGTON
May 1991

YORK May 1991

LEEDS
Oct 1989

DONCASTER
Oct 1989

PETERBOROUGH
May 1987

HUNTINGDON
May 1987

LONDON
KING'S
CROSS

Perhaps the most exciting development for railways in the future is the construction of the cross-channel link. The idea for such a link is not a new one. This picture shows the proposal of a Frenchman in 1802.

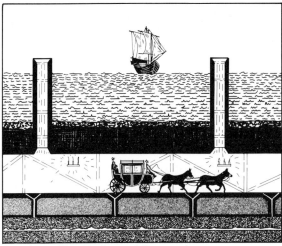

C What problems do you think there might be if this proposal had been used to build a cross-channel link?

In 1985, businesses were invited to submit schemes for building a cross-channel link. The three main contenders were:

Channel Tunnel Group — a twin rail shuttle to destinations like Paris and Brussels.
Euro Route — bridges to man-made islands,which are connected by a tunnel across the middle of the Channel.
Channel Expressway — twin tunnels mainly for road traffic.
The governments of Britain and France made their decision in January, 1986.

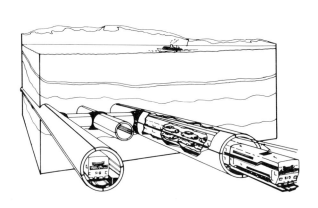

Artist's impression of the winning scheme

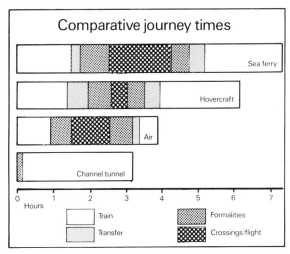

Autumn 1985	January 1986	1987	1990	1991	1992	Spring 1993
Businesses invited to submit channel link schemes	Governments make the decision	Construction begins	Service tunnel completed	Main tunnel completed	Fitting out of tunnel	Operations begin

Channel tunnel time line

D 1 Look at the artist's impression of the link. Which of the schemes won?
   2 Look at the comparative journey times. How much faster will the tunnel crossing be?
   3 Look at the time line. How long will the tunnels take to build from the idea in 1985 until the actual opening?
   4 In what ways do you think that Britain will benefit from a cross-channel link?

Investigating

Private Railways

Railway museums seek to restore and preserve engines and carriages. Private railways also want to do this, but to them putting life back into steam railways is of special importance; they want people to see them working and to travel on them. Today, there are over 50 of these private railways in Britain.

kwvlr Keighley & Worth Valley Railway

WEST SOMERSET RAILWAY

STRATHSPEY RAILWAY

**KENT & EAST SUSSEX RAILWAY
TENTERDEN TOWN STATION
TENTERDEN
KENT TN30 6HE
TELEPHONE (05806) 5155**

With the Compliments of

The Bluebell Railway

The Keighley and Worth Valley Railway is owned, managed and operated by volunteers. It is a complex undertaking. Jobs to be done range from locomotive maintenance to running a shop. Some tasks are carried out by newcomers, but others require specialist skills which take years to acquire.

Since 1968 about two million people have visited the Keighley and Worth Valley Railway for a variety of reasons.

Activities

A Make a list of the reasons these people gave for coming to the Railway.

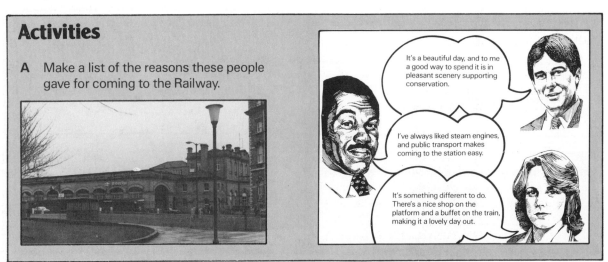

It's a beautiful day, and to me a good way to spend it is in pleasant scenery supporting conservation.

I've always liked steam engines, and public transport makes coming to the station easy.

It's something different to do. There's a nice shop on the platform and a buffet on the train, making it a lovely day out.

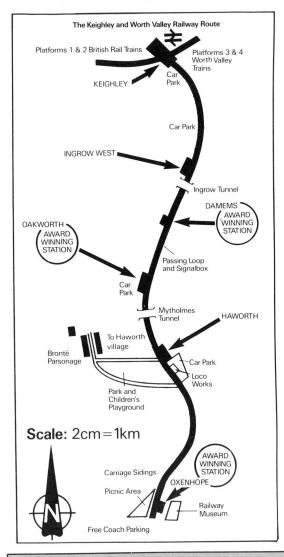

The Keighley and Worth Valley Railway Route

Platforms 1 & 2 British Rail Trains
Platforms 3 & 4 Worth Valley Trains
KEIGHLEY
Car Park
Car Park
INGROW WEST
Ingrow Tunnel
DAMEMS AWARD WINNING STATION
OAKWORTH AWARD WINNING STATION
Passing Loop and Signalbox
Car Park
Mytholmes Tunnel
HAWORTH
To Haworth village
Brontë Parsonage
Car Park
Loco Works
Park and Children's Playground

Scale: 2cm = 1km

Carriage Sidings
Picnic Area
AWARD WINNING STATION
OXENHOPE
Railway Museum
Free Coach Parking
N

How people heard of the Railway.

Mentioned by friends/relatives	ⅢⅠ ⅢⅠ ⅢⅠ ⅢⅠ ‖
Posters/timetables advertising the Railway	‖‖
TV/radio/newspapers	ⅢⅠ ‖
Tourist Information Office	ⅢⅠ ⅢⅠ ⅢⅠ Ⅰ
Came across the Railway by accident	‖‖
Always known about it	ⅢⅠ ⅢⅠ ⅢⅠ ⅢⅠ ⅢⅠ ⅢⅠ
Other reasons	Ⅰ

B
1. About how long is the Keighley and Worth Railway route?
2. How many stations are there along the line?
3. Draw a bar graph to show the results of Class 8's questionnaire on how people had heard of the railway.
4. How had most people heard of the Railway?
5. People were also asked where they came from to visit the Keighley and Worth Valley Railway. Write a few sentences describing their results which are shown on the graph opposite.

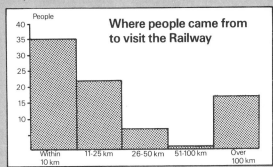

Where people came from to visit the Railway

People
40
35
30
25
20
15
10

Within 10 km   11-25 km   26-50 km   51-100 km   Over 100 km

C   Investigate your local private railway. Here are some suggestions for information to collect: Try to find out why people have come to the railway, how they heard of it and where they came from. You can compare your results with those above.
Also interview staff to find out what they do for the railway. Sketch, take photographs and collect any written information about the railway that you can.

Sample Worksheets

Line		Ref.		Section length	km
Feature	Number	Sketch	Ref.	Notes
Viaducts				
Bridges				
Cuttings				
Embankments				
Tunnels				
Total				

Investigating Railway buildings, page 7.

		Region		Period covered		
News number/ Rail service	Cancellation — why?	Delays — how long/why?	Buses replace — from/to	Diversions — to where?	Stations missed	Other reason

Investigating Railway Maintenance, page 19.

Station		Name	
Comfort facility	Score 0-5	Comments	
Station cleanliness			
Waiting room			
Refreshments			
Bookstall			
Luggage trolleys			
Seating			
Toilets			
Left luggage			
Telephones			
Others, please list:			
Information facility checklist			
Poster timetable			
Video timetable			
Announcer			
Enquiry office			
Information person			
Interview 1			
Interview 2			
Interview 3			

Investigating Train journeys, page 22.

Notes for Teachers

AIMS This book aims to:

- provide stimulus material which will lead children into studying railways in their environment.

- develop the skills listed below through direct observation, practical investigation and information gathering and sorting.

- develop powers of deduction so that railways can be interpreted from visual evidence.

- suggest ideas so that opinions can be formed as to the impact of railways on the environment.

- provide a background vocabulary and knowledge from which to do this.

SKILLS This book helps children to develop skills in:

- using photographs and diagrams as sources of information.

- conducting field surveys in order to gather information.

- the practical use of maps at a variety of levels.

- using mathematics to help describe real-life situations.

- report writing.

- gaining a balanced view of the available information and avoiding over-commitment to any one explanation of it.

CONCEPTS This book leads children towards developing concepts about:

- the relationship between landscape and railway networks.

- the role of railways as a source of transport for industry and leisure past and present.

- the importance of technology in railway development.

- the organization of modern railways as a complex undertaking.

- the importance of railway conservation in recognizing man's achievements and maintaining interest in railway developments.

- continuity and change in British railways.

ATTITUDES AND VALUES The work in this book should foster:

- an attitude of curiosity which prompts inquiry into railways.

- a willingness to change a point of view in the face of evidence, and a readiness to suspend a conclusion, when information gathered shows inconsistency or lack of general pattern.

- a desire to probe more deeply for reasons and explanations and not merely to accept an unsubstantiated thought.

- an attitude which accepts differences in interpretations which in turn provoke reflection on observations and further thinking on the issues.

Implementation

USING THIS BOOK

Each section provides sufficient material to allow work to be undertaken solely from the book. Using the ideas and material in these pages, teachers can lead children into investigations and interpretations immediately in the classroom. However, the intention is that children should venture out into their own environment and pursue the kind of research that the different sections suggest. Background vocabulary and classification knowledge is given, so that children can move into the essence of their work directly and without the distractions and frustrations that fieldwork can so often incur.

MIXED ABILITY

The work is designed to cater for children of all abilities working in the same class. The information given is of easy readability and the tasks and field techniques suggested are clear and straightforward. The development of the investigations allows active participation by the least able, whilst the most able children are led into very challenging situations. Theories and hypotheses are usually neither right nor wrong, rather there are solutions which are more or less acceptable depending upon the quality and reliability of the evidence and the judgement upon which they are based. The better the evidence then, the stronger the work will be. It is of great educational value if children can themselves find evidence to support their view, but, at the same time, be aware of any weaknesses, shortcomings and inconsistencies in it.

At all ability levels children should be encouraged throughout this work to seek out patterns of: (i) similarity and difference; (ii) continuity and change; (iii) cause and effect.

PAGE BY PAGE

7   A 1:50,000 map is best for exercise B, although a traced map extract of a similar scale, layer shaded, may need to be used with younger children. Background information on local railway links is useful here.

9   Modern fares, times, etc. are taken from scheduled services, not excursions. Information on catering etc. is also useful for comparison.

14   A full list of station closures can be found in 'The Re-shaping of British Railways' — British Railways Board — HMSO Stations and holts due for closure before Beeching are not included in the map of Northamptonshire.

15   Permission should be obtained from property owners before a visit is made. New uses of 'axed' stations can be discovered by talking to parents, visiting libraries and newspaper offices, as well as the old stations themselves.

16   A station visit may be arranged to include a tour of signalling areas. Station Managers of the larger stations may organise this.

19   'Oracle' (ITV's Teletext) may be used in this investigation, although information here tends to be less specific. Initially, engineering information should be placed on a large class map.

22   A preliminary visit is a useful aid to constructing the survey sheet and station plan.
     Permission will need to be obtained from the Station Manager prior to a class visit.

25   Information can be collected on the various cross-channel schemes.

27   It is wise to inform the railway in advance of a visit. A trip on the train provides a worthwhile focal point to the exercise.

ORGANIZATION OF TIME

Good fieldwork takes time and so does good follow-up work. Whilst the work needs to have pace and development, it does require blocks of time that extend beyond the conventional 'lesson period'. Given this, the children should, by working from Investigating Railways, develop a critical awareness and understanding beyond the ambitions of many topic-book approaches.

Consultation with many teachers and advisers has revealed the need for a series which helps to structure topic work in the local environment. Structured investigations into the child's own environment can be a rich source of ideas and motivation leading to work in other disciplines. Each book in the series has the following aims:

- to provide sufficient information and structure for pupils, either individually or in groups, to carry out their own investigations into their environment;

- to provide, for those pupils who are unable to go outside the classroom, sufficient information for them to be able to experience the key ideas concerning the local environment;

- to provide for the teacher a set of structured ideas for investigating the environment.

    Details of all these and other titles can be found in the Arnold-Wheaton catalogue.